# The Color of ME

# The Outside of Me

# The Inside of Me

My Name

# My Family

Dear Mom —

Dear Dad –

# My Dreams

*Imagine*

Create

# My Nightmares

# My Nightmares

# My Songs

# My Poetry

Create

Write

*Imagine*

_Speak_

Shout

# My Favorite Colors

red    purple    pink
orange    green    blue
yellow    black

# SAFE

Remember, we all stumble, every one of us. That's why it's a comfort to go hand in hand.

- Emily Kimbrough

SAFE

Remember, we all stumble, every one of us. That's why it's a comfort to go hand in hand.

Emily Kimbrough

# My Safety

# Safe People

# Safe People

# Safe Places

# Safe Places

# Safe Words

# Safe Words

# Safe Images

# Safe Images

# Safe Touch

Safe Touch

LIFE

Tell me, what is it you plan
to do with your one wild and
precious life? – Mary Oliver

Beautiful
Girl

# My Timeline

## Place I was born

# Where I am today

# FEEL

*Don't ask yourself what the world needs. Ask yourself what makes you come alive and then go do that. Because what the world needs is people who have come alive.*

- Howard Thurman

FEEL

Don't ask yourself what the world needs. Ask yourself what makes you come alive and then go do that. Because what the world needs is people who have come alive.

—Howard Thurman

# My feelings

*I feel mad when ...*

angry

bothered                                    irked

disgusted                                       ruffled

*I feel enraged when ...*

*I feel jealous when ...*

*I feel furious when ...*

*I feel sad when ...*

melancholy       low       blue

worn out       down

*I feel crushed when ...*

hurt

disappointed

somber

*I feel miserable about ...*

unhappy

melancholy

depressed

*I feel defeated when ...*

mournful

gloomy                                    grieved

dissatisfied

*I feel empty when ...*

lousy          despairing

devastated                    crushed

*I feel worn out when ...*

defeated

dejected

miserable

wretched

empty

*I feel glad about ...*

warm

comfortable

grateful

cheerful

refreshed

relaxed

*I feel refreshed when ...*

proud

tickled       hopeful

happy     optimistic     contented

delighted

*I feel loved when ...*

thrilled

encouraged

pleased

*I feel clean when ...*

exhilarated

refreshed          satisfied

elated

*I feel worthy and valued when ...*

ecstatic   overjoyed

joyful

*I feel afraid when ...*

overwhelmed

careful

shocked          apprehensive

uneasy

*I feel anxious about ...*

cautious                    vulnerable
        agitated                    scared

    hesitant                      tense

*I feel overwhelmed when ...*

frightened                              alarmed

        repulsed
edgy                    nervous            distressed

                    anxious

*I feel panicked about ...*

horrified      frantic      panic stricken

terrified      numb      petrified

*I feel confused when ...*

curious          ambivalent

uncertain

*I feel distrustful when ...*

jumbled

doubtful

hesitant

unsettled     dismayed     insecure

baffled     distracted

*I feel fragmented when ...*

unfocused        puzzled     torn

perplexed    muddled    flustered

fragmented

*I feel chaotic when ...*

chaotic

bewildered

stunned

dazed

lost

# I feel ashamed about ...

awkward

self-conscious

clumsy

*I feel guilty when ...*

flustered                                    embarrassed
disconcerted

abashed

*I feel violated when ...*

guilty     regretful     ashamed

sorry     belittled     apologetic

remorseful

*I feel exploited when ...*

violated

defiled

dirty    humiliated                    mortified

degraded.

devastated

*I feel lonely when ...*

out of place     left out

lonesome

*I feel unwelcome when ...*

removed

insignificant                                        unappreciated

neglected            disconnected

unwanted

insecure

*I feel ignored when ...*

isolated

detached

misunderstood

excluded

ignored

unwelcome

invisible

# I feel unwanted when ...

rejected

abandoned

deserted    forsaken

outcast                    withdrawn

desolate

*Being unwanted, unloved, uncared for, forgotten by everybody. I think that is a much greater hunger, a much greater poverty than the person who has nothing to eat.*

- Mother Teresa

ART

Being unwanted, unloved, uncared for, forgotten by everybody, I think that is a much greater hunger, a much greater poverty than the person who has nothing to eat.

-Mother Teresa

# My Hurt

# People who hurt me

# People who help me

# Things I give away

# Things that others give to me

# Places where
# I've been hurt

# Places where
# I've been helped

*Words that make me cry*

*Words that
make me feel loved*

# Images that keep me awake

*Images that*
*make me feel safe*

*Touch that hurts*

Touch that comforts

Na!

Yes!

# TREASURE

Precious jewel,
You glow,
You shine,
Reflecting all the good
Things in the world.
Just look at yourself!

- Maya Angelou

TREASURE

Precious jewel,
Open glow,
Open shine,
Reflecting all the good
things in the world.
Just look at yourself.

-Maya Angelou

# Treasure

*I am a treasure*

*I am a miracle*

*I am loved*

# Fearless

*Free*

Trust again

*Strong*

*Soft*

Lead

Future

Fabulous

# Peace

*Hope*

Beauty

Dream

*Imagine*

Create

Breathe

*You inspire*